The Beauty and Peace in Grace

Susan Leffler

Written and Illustrated by Susan Leffler
Inspired by the Holy Spirit

Unless otherwise noted, all Scripture is taken from
the New King James Version.
Copyright 1982 by Thomas Nelson, Inc.
Used by permission.
All rights reserved.

Author's Note

This is the fifth and final book in the series of Gracie. The number five means grace and little did I realize that I would end up writing five books about Gracie! God has a way of slipping those kinds of things in without you knowing it until later. God is so good!
I love it when He does that.

God has blessed me by giving me this little character, Gracie. By looking at God through the eyes of a child you can plainly see God is love. He is good. He is beautiful. He is your peace, your joy, your strength. He is your all in all. Through a child's eyes you just accept and believe in Him. No questions asked. You believe His word because it is truth - no ifs, ands or buts!

These books were written for everyone, young and old. My hope in what you take away from Gracie and this series is that God is not complicated. God loved us so much that He gave His Son Jesus to save us. Jesus is the Word, He is the Life, He is the Truth and He is the only way to the Father and eternal life.

It's simple. Only believe!

Hi! My name is Grace, but everyone calls me 'Gracie'.

This is Oscar, my puppy. Isn't he beautiful?

That's what I want to tell you about,
the beauty and peace of God.

God created everything with beauty,
from the little ant to the big elephant.

All of God's creatures are beautiful.

Then God saw everything that He had made, and indeed it *was* very good.

Genesis 1:31

You and I are God's creations.

Even when we wake up in the morning,
before we comb our hair and brush our teeth and
get dressed; God sees us as His beautiful creations.

For I know the thoughts that I think toward you, says the LORD,
thoughts of peace and not of evil, to give you a future and a hope.

Jeremiah 29:11

For the LORD takes pleasure in His people;
He will beautify the humble with salvation.

Psalm 149:4

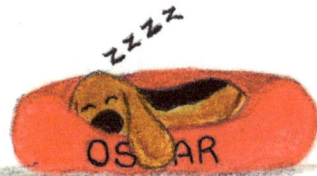

God doesn't look at your outward appearance; He looks at your heart. Not your physical heart, but your spirit.

You were made in the image of God. God is a spirit.
You are a spirit. But God also gave you a soul.
Your soul is your personality, your thoughts and emotions.
Your body is the house that your spirit and soul live in!
You are a spirit that has a soul that lives in a body.

For the LORD does not see as man sees; for man looks at the outward appearance, but the LORD looks at the heart.
1 Samuel 16:7

So God created man in His own image; in the image of God He created him; male and female He created them.
Genesis 1:27

Now may the God of peace Himself sanctify you completely; and may your whole spirit, soul, and body be preserved blameless at the coming of our Lord Jesus Christ.
1 Thessalonians 5:23

God is Spirit, and those who worship Him must worship in spirit and truth.
John 4:24

...rather let it be the hidden person of the heart, with the incorruptible beauty of a gentle and quiet spirit, which is very precious in the sight of God.
1 Peter 3:4

Soul

Body

Spirit

MIND
WILL
EMOTIONS

Jesus gives you His peace and places it in your spirit.
The peace that Jesus gives you comes from the inside out.
It's kind of like the purr of a kitten.

But the fruit of the Spirit is love, joy, peace, longsuffering, kindness,
goodness, faithfulness, gentleness, self-control.

Galatians 5:22-23

I was mute with silence, I held my peace even from good; And my sorrow was stirred up.

Psalm 39:2

But let patience have its perfect work, that you may be perfect and complete, lacking nothing.

James 1:4

Jesus is called the Prince of Peace.
Jesus will give you His peace when you ask Him
to come into your heart. You can't get that kind of peace
from anywhere else. You have that peace wherever you go
because Jesus said He will never leave you.

Peace I leave with you, My peace I give to you; not as the world gives do I give to you.
Let not your heart be troubled, neither let it be afraid.

John 14:27

For He himself has said, "I will never leave you nor forsake you."

Hebrews 13:5

When you have God's peace, you begin to see God's beauty.

Sometimes I sit out in the garden and look
at all the beauty that God has created and how
He made everything with a purpose and how
everything works together.

I will meditate on the glorious splendor of Your majesty, and on Your wondrous works.

Psalm 145:5

God displays all His wisdom and beauty
in everything He created.

Look at the flowers, they are not only beautiful,
but they also provide food for the bees. And the bees
make honey that provide food for us (and the bears)!

O LORD, how manifold are Your works! In wisdom You have made them all.
The earth is full of Your possessions.

Psalm 104:24

...Look now, how my countenance has brightened because I tasted a little of this honey.

1 Samuel 14:29

If God provides food for the bees and birds
and all the animals then you shouldn't worry
but have peace in knowing that when you put God
first in your life, God will provide for you too!

Look at the birds of the air, for they neither sow nor reap nor gather into barns;
yet your heavenly Father feeds them. Are you not of more value than they?

Matthew 6:26

Therefore do not worry, saying, 'What shall we eat?'
or 'What shall we drink?' or 'What shall we wear?'

Matthew 6:31

But seek first the kingdom of God and His righteousness,
and all these things shall be added to you.

Matthew 6:33

I think all things God created are beautiful
and He enjoys them as much as we do.

He has made everything beautiful in its time.

Ecclesiastes 3:11

And one cried to another and said: "Holy, holy, holy is the LORD of hosts;
The whole earth is full of His glory!"

Isaiah 6:3

Thou art worthy, O Lord, to receive glory and honour and power; for thou hast
created all things, and for thy pleasure they are and were created.

Revelation 4:11 (KJV)

Stand still and consider the wondrous works of God.

Job 37:14

When God finished creating the heavens and earth
and all living creatures, He saw that it was all good.
So He rested on the seventh day. God wasn't tired;
He just finished creating everything
that needed to be created!

And on the seventh day God ended His work which He had done,
and He rested on the seventh day from all His work which he had done.
Then God blessed the seventh day and sanctified it, because in it
He rested from all His work which God had created and made.

Genesis 2:2-3

When Jesus was here on earth, He fulfilled
all of the prophesies that were spoken of Him
in the Old Testament. Jesus said, "It is finished."
Jesus accomplished everything that He was sent
here to earth to do. Jesus went to heaven and sat
down at the right hand of God, and He rested.

But this Man, after He had offered one sacrifice for sins forever,
sat down at the right hand of God...

Hebrews 10:12

Then He said to them, "These are the words which I spoke to you
while I was still with you, that all things must be fulfilled which were written
in the Law of Moses and the Prophets and the Psalms concerning me.

Luke 24:44

But those things which God foretold by the mouth of all His prophets,
that the Christ would suffer, He has thus fulfilled.

Acts 3:18

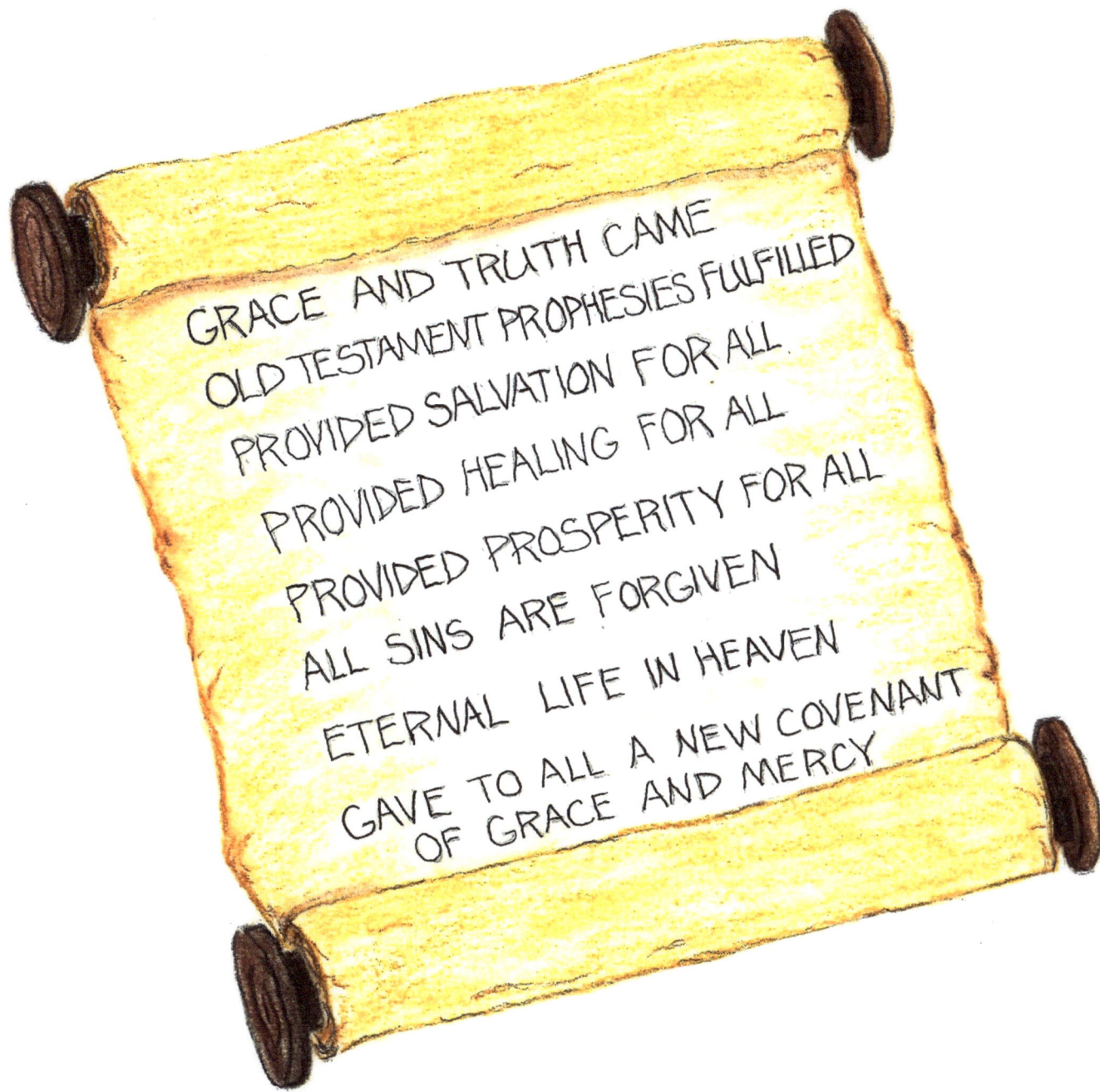

GRACE AND TRUTH CAME

OLD TESTAMENT PROPHESIES FULFILLED

PROVIDED SALVATION FOR ALL

PROVIDED HEALING FOR ALL

PROVIDED PROSPERITY FOR ALL

ALL SINS ARE FORGIVEN

ETERNAL LIFE IN HEAVEN

GAVE TO ALL A NEW COVENANT
OF GRACE AND MERCY

To know the peace that Jesus gives you is for
you to rest in what He accomplished on the cross.
Jesus wants you to rest in knowing that everything
you need has already been provided for you.
You don't need to worry about anything. He wants
you to give all your cares and worry to Him.

You are of God, little children, and have overcome them, because He who is in
you is greater than he who is in the world.

1 John 4:4

Therefore humble yourselves under the mighty hand of God, that He may
exalt you in due time, casting all your care upon Him, for He cares for you.

1 Peter 5:6-7

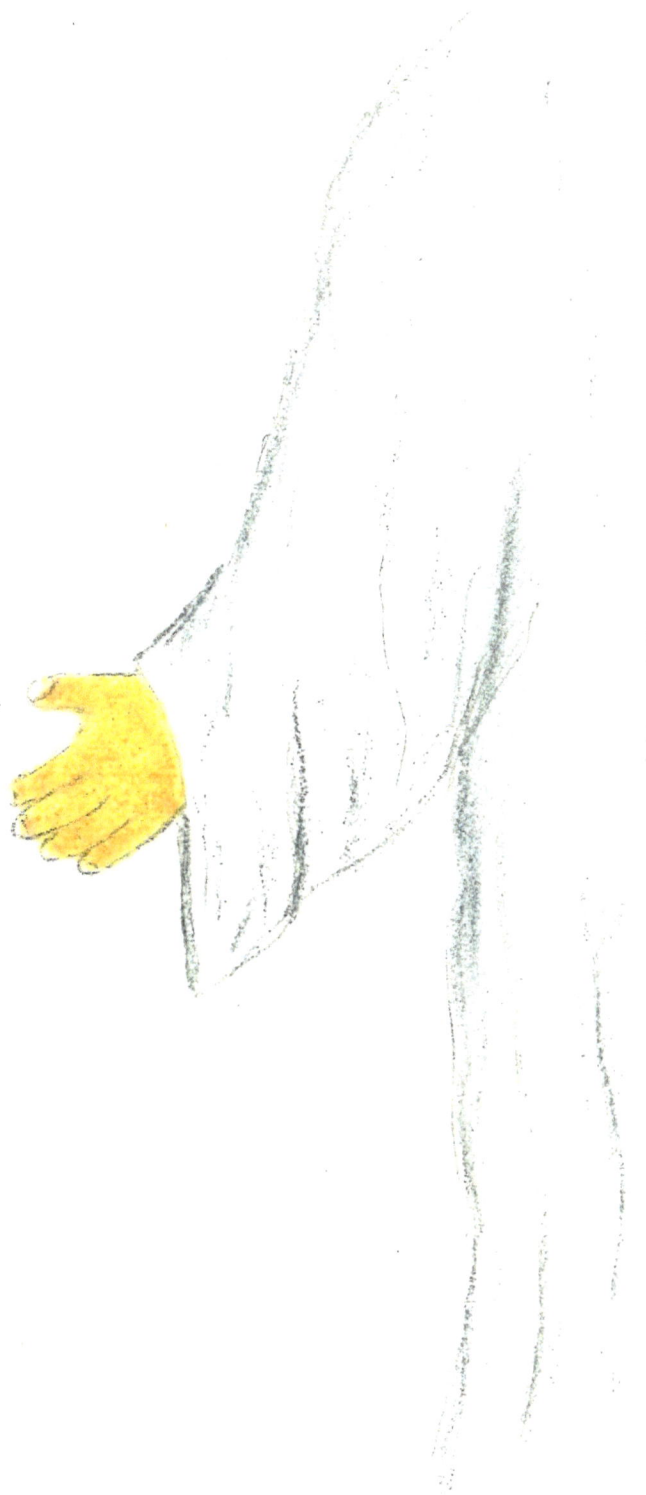

I once said to God, "Papa, even though I can't see You face to face, I see Your beauty all around me."

And God said, "Gracie, I don't need to look any further than your heart to see yours."

One thing I have desired of the LORD, That will I seek: That I may dwell in the house of the LORD All the days of my life, To behold the beauty of the LORD...

Psalm 27:4

Now may the Lord of peace Himself give you peace always in every way. The LORD be with you all.

2 Thessalonians 3:16

Accepting Jesus

To know love is to know Jesus. And to know Jesus is to know God the Father, because God is love. If you want to know Jesus and the Father's love, ask Him into your life. He will show you and tell you all about His love and all the gifts He has made available for you, just like He did with me. Just say;

"Jesus, I believe in my heart you are the Son of God and that you were raised from the dead and sit at the right hand of God the Father. I ask you to be my Lord and Savior. I ask you into my life and I receive my salvation now. Thank you Jesus for saving me."

Receive the Baptism of the Holy Spirit

If you just said that prayer and accepted Jesus into your life,
or if Jesus is already part of your life, then God the Father
wants to give you His Holy Spirit.

The Holy Spirit will live in you and will guide you
and teach you in the way of Father God.
All you have to do is ask, believe and receive. Just say;

"Father, I ask for your power and your guidance
to live this new life you have for me. Please fill me
with your Holy Spirit. I receive Him right now.
Thank you for baptizing me with your Holy Spirit."

Susan and Chris Leffler are founders of Finished Works Ministry. You may contact them at,

Finishedworksministry@hotmail.com